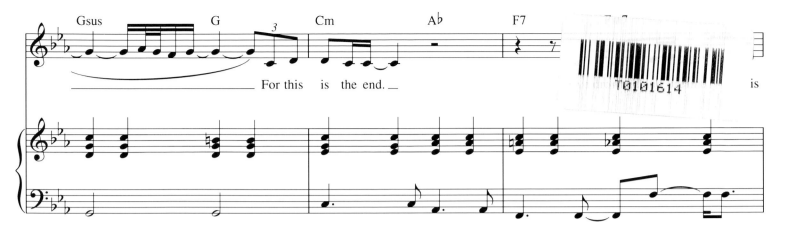

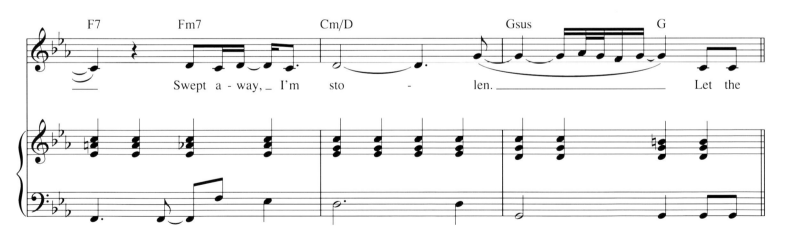

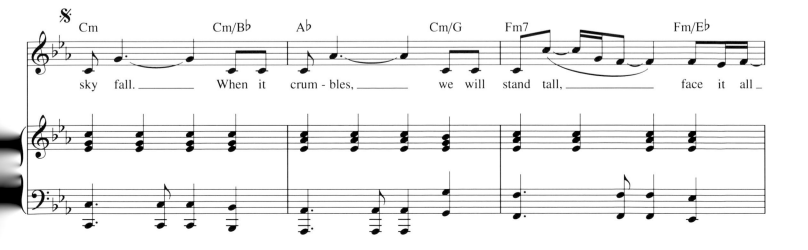

to-geth-er. Let the sky fall._____ When it crum-bles,_____ we will

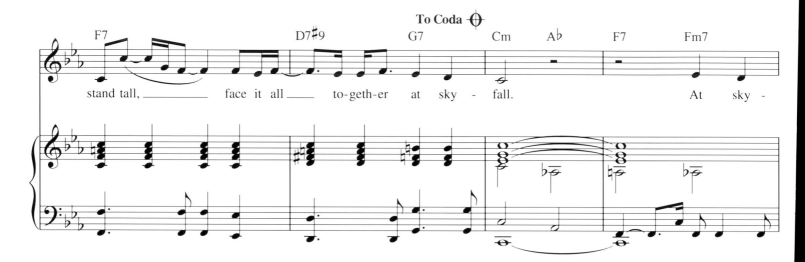

To Coda ⊕

stand tall,_____ face it all___ to-geth-er at sky - fall._____ At sky -

fall. Sky-fall is where __ we start,_____ a thou-sand miles __ and

poles a - part. _ When worlds col-lide __ and days are dark._____ You may have my

I see. I know I'll nev-er be ___ me ___ with-out the se-cu-ri-ty ___ of your

lov-ing arms ___ keep-ing me from harm. ___ Put your hand ___ in my hand ___ and we'll

stand. _____ Let the sky fall. _____ When it crum-bles, _____ we will

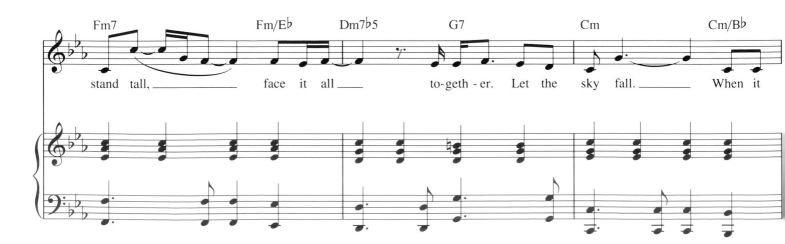

stand tall, _____ face it all ___ to-geth-er. Let the sky fall. _____ When it

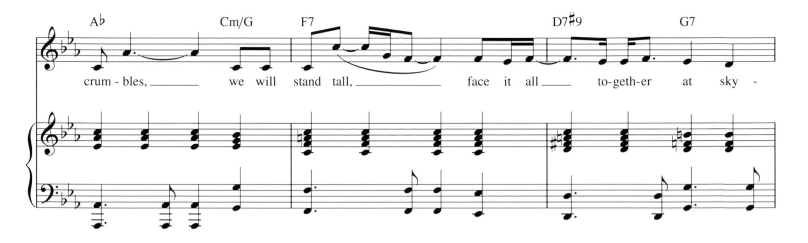

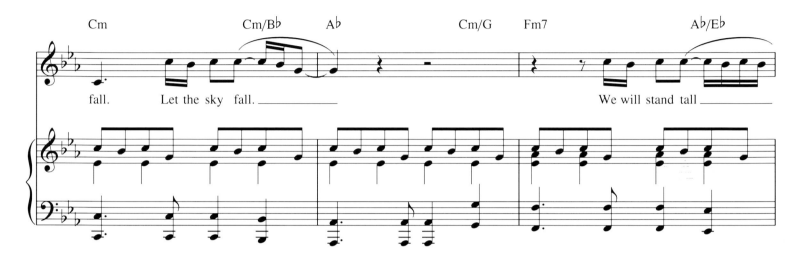

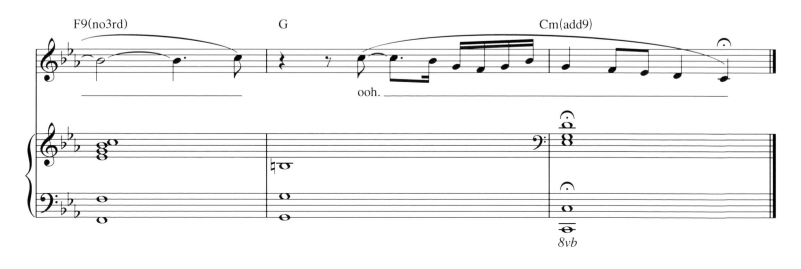

Also available:

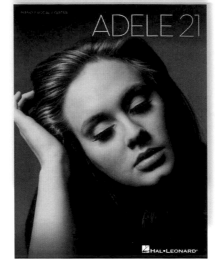

19
Piano/Vocal/GuitarSongbook   00307038 $17.99

21
Piano/Vocal/Guitar Songbook   00307247 $17.99

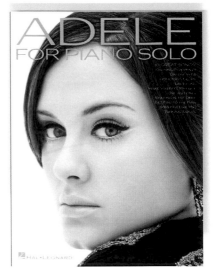

ADELE FOR PIANO SOLO
Piano Solo Songbook   00307585 $12.99

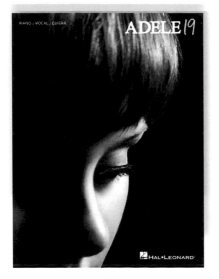

JAMES BOND FAQ
Reference Book   00314951 $22.99

CHASING PAVEMENTS
Piano/Vocal/Guitar Sheet   00353919 $3.99

ROLLING IN THE DEEP
Piano/Vocal/Guitar Sheet   00354175 $3.99

SOMEONE LIKE YOU
Piano/Vocal/Guitar Sheet   00354227 $3.99

SET FIRE TO THE RAIN
Piano/Vocal/Guitar Sheet   00354263 $3.99

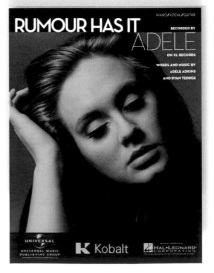

RUMOUR HAS IT
Piano/Vocal/Guitar Sheet   00354299 $3.99